Dear Ron,

20 years of free advice,
whether people wanted it or not.

Ron Dentinger

ISBN: 1456330012
ISBN-13: 9781456330019

Who gives advice to Dear Abby's Abigail Van Buren? And who gives advice to Dr. Phil, and to the members of Congress and to Bret Favre? Who cares? However, if you want to know who gives advice to the readers of the Dodgeville Chronicle...that would be Ron Dentinger.

"Dear Ron," is taken from twenty years of advice that was offered "free" to the readers of the Dodgeville Chronicle. In that time there have been only a few divorces and about a half dozen lawsuits as a result of people using the advice in Ron's column. Who's to say that those divorces and lawsuits would not have happened anyway?

About the author

Ron Dentinger has spent over 25 years traveling from coast-to-coast on the banquet circuit, entertaining for corporation and association banquets. Ron also does some concert-stage work as the "Opening Act" for many nationally known performers.

In addition to working the banquet circuit and stage shows, he has also sold jokes to some of the all-time comedy greats, including the late Rodney Dangerfield.

Ron has accumulated what has to be the largest humor library of its kind anywhere in the country. It includes several thousand books, magazines, videos, CDs and DVDs. The items span 250 years covering all aspects of humor and the ongoing evolution of humor.

For 20+ years he was the person the late Paul Harvey quoted most often when he closed his broadcasts with: "And now, for what it's worth…" then he would say, "Dodgeville Wisconsin's, Ron Dentinger, says…." and he would use one of the lines from Ron's column.

And then, after 70 years of broadcasting, on what would be his final broadcast…Paul Harvey quoted Ron one more time, and said, "Paul Harvey….good day." for the last time.

(www.banquetspeaker.com – 608-574-6924)

Dedicated to...

I would like to thank my daughter, Joann, and her husband, Dave, for donating a room in their home to house my humor library, and also for putting up with the humor library's administrator, who came along with the whole "Humor Library Package" thing and has taken up sanctuary in the Green Room.

I would also like to thank my daughter-in-law, Tricia Sue, for putting up with my son, Ron, Jr., and for giving me two wonderful grandchildren: Ron Lee and Tricia Ann. And I especially thank my son and his family for proving that family values can actually still be found.

I would like to thank (blame?) my father, R.I.P., who had a great sense of humor, and my mother, for all the years of putting up with my father and his great sense of humor.

I would like to thank the teachers for putting up with my brother and me. They once pooled their money and offered to buy my father a vasectomy.

This book is a frivolous quick read.

It's a great book to put on the night stand in a guest room.

It's a great book for under the short leg of a wobbly table.

And it is a great gift for that person you feel obligated to buy a gift for, but don't like enough to spend more than ten bucks on.

It is not a bathroom type reader, although my publisher says that it could have been, back in the good old days when we used outhouses and Sears Roebuck catalogs.

A reader writes:

Dear Ron,

I subscribe to the belief that a man's home is his castle. What about you?

Signed, HP

Dear HP,

There was a time I subscribed to the belief that a man's home is his castle, and then one day my wife cancelled my subscription.

A reader writes:

Dear Ron,

My wife and I are thinking about getting a dog for a pet. Is it best to get a smaller dog for a house pet?

Signed, TM

Dear TM,

Yes, a small dog would be good. Just don't get one so small that you have to lift it up every time it wants a drink out of the toilet.

A reader writes:

Dear Ron,

I read that the Mormon Church abolished polygamy in 1890, but it didn't say why they abolished polygamy.

Do you know why polygamy was abolished?

Signed, CW

Dear CW,

I think I know why. It's my understanding that one of the Mormon prophets was able to see into the future and he foresaw the coming of credit cards.

A reader writes:

Dear Ron,

Most marriage services are in the morning. Is there a reason most couples get married in the morning?

Signed, JB

Dear JB,

It's best if you get married in the morning. That way if the marriage doesn't work out, you don't ruin the entire day.

A reader writes:

Dear Ron,

I read over 11,000 accidents occur in the home every day. Who comes up with these statistics?

Signed, WP

Dear WP,

My guess would be it is probably those people at the Planned Parenthood Federation.

A reader writes:

Dear Ron,

I notice that I haven't seen the Energizer Bunny for quite a while. What happened to him?

Signed, LR

Dear LR,

It's very sad. I'm told the bunny accidentally wound up on the street out in front of the 122nd National Rifle Association Convention. They say there wasn't enough left of that little bunny to make a Q-Tip.

A reader writes:

Dear Ron,

A brick hit the front windshield on my car. Until it's fixed, what can I do to keep the wind from hitting me in the face when I drive to the mall?

Signed, Francine

Dear Francine,

You might try backing your car to the mall.

A reader writes:

Dear Ron,

My two year old son is eating his crayons. Any idea how I can stop him?

Signed, MT

Dear MT,

I would suggest that you tell the little guy that crayons are good for him.

A reader writes:

Dear Ron,

Do you have any advice as to how I might pick up a date?

Signed, TM

Dear TM,

Yes I do. If you feel that you would like to pick up a date, I'd recommend that you bend at the knees and keep your back straight.

A reader writes:

Dear Ron,

I read an article today claiming men are twice as likely to fall out of a hospital bed as women are. Why is that?

Signed, PJ

Dear PJ,

That's probably because the men are twice as likely to reach out and try to grab a nurse.

A reader writes:

Dear Ron,

What wine do you suggest goes the best with Chicken Cacciatore?

Signed, JR

Dear JR,

Forget wine. Try something a little different. Blend some chicken gizzards in a blender with a couple shots of rum, a slice of lime, and pour it over ice in a champagne glass. Then you'll enjoy your Chicken Cacciatore with a nice Chicken Cacciadaiquiri.

A reader writes:

Dear Ron,

I don't think I'm going to like the changes in the new health care plan. Today I got a bill for watching Dr. Phil."

Signed, RM

Dear RM.

I've had my fill of Dr. Phil.

FYI: I have just analyzed the wording in the dental coverage for Senior Citizens on the new health care plan. Briefly summarized it is: "Chew on the other side."

∽○

Is humor good for a person?

Does Wendy Williams like to talk?

A reader writes:

Dear Ron,

I'm not able to find the origin of the word "flabbergasted" and I've looked everywhere. Can you help?

Signed, TP"

Dear TP,

I think that you are flabbergasted when you are gasted by a flabber. The problem here is that I have no idea what a flabber is.

For that matter, gasted has me puzzled too. And as for the origin of flabbergasted....my guess is that it is Norwegian. It sounds Norwegian doesn't it? It also sounds painful. Example: "Uff dah! I think I was just flabbergasted."

A government study claims that more people are allergic to cats than to dogs.

And they feel cats are not only aware of this ... the cats are actually proud of it.

Another government study has determined that the nail on the toe next to the big toe grows faster than the nails on any of the other toes.

Don't you sometimes wonder just how much the government pays for these studies?

A reader writes:

Dear Ron,

I notice that our brand new hardwood floor is starting to squeak when I walk on it.

What do you suggest I can do about it?

Signed, TR

Dear TR,

If you really want to know....I suggest that you stop going back for seconds.

A reader writes:

Dear Ron,

Which do you think is longer, the NBA regular season or the NBA playoffs?

Signed, BB

Dear BB,

My guess is…the NBA playoffs are longer than the regular season, because I am pretty sure that there are more teams playing in the NBA playoffs than in the regular season.

You don't have to worry much about the world coming to an end. They can't even bring the NBA basketball season to an end.

A reader writes:

Dear Ron,

I say, "Why should we ban guns. Guns don't kill people. People kill people."

Signed, VJ

Dear VJ,

I read your comment three times and I'm wondering… are you suggesting that we ban people?

Correction:

Last week we reported on a new government survey that determined that men like cooking more than women.

What we meant to say is: "Men like cooking more than women like cooking."

Correction:

In last week's paper we offered a suggestion for married men who are looking to improve the relationship in their marriage. However, we inadvertently used the word "fake."

Our intention was to suggest men should "take" an interest in their spouse's concerns.

A reader writes:

Dear Ron,

There are some things that a wife just doesn't understand. For example…we were packing to go on our camping trip and I asked my wife to pack something to clean the fish and she packed a bar of soap.

Signed, Ralph

Dear Ralph,

I hear ya. Women don't like to go camping. My wife says the worst part about camping is when you are in your sleeping bag, and are just about to drift off to sleep, and you notice that the itch on your leg is moving.

A reader wrote asking for any suggestions that I might have to stop a 6-year-old from wetting the bed.

At first I thought the kid was a typical bed wetter, but he is not a typical bed wetter. This kid has been wetting the bed from on top of the dresser.

Another reader wrote: "Halloween is the only time I understand the way kids dress."

A reader writes:

Dear Ron,

There has been a lot of talk about whether various human behaviors are environmental or genetic and I find it to be very confusing. Can you help?

Signed, GW

Dear GW,

Yes, it's confusing, but I think I can explain what things are caused by genetics and what things are caused by the environment.

If your baby looks like the father, then that would be genetic. However, if the baby looks like the neighbor, that's environment.

Regarding typos and corrections:

In Earle Tempel's book "Press Boners" Tempel notes that even the Chicago Tribune makes errors. Like the time they printed this correction:

"Unfortunately, the illustrations of the edible and the poisonous types of mushrooms were reversed on Page 14 of our Sunday edition."

A reader wrote to say that he traced his roots and was very surprised to learn that he is one-third French, and one-third Italian, and one-third Thousand Island.

A reader writes:

Dear Ron,

Are you aware that we have a gang problem in our city? The gangs roam around wearing green berets and they intimidate people into giving them money.

Signed, TR

Dear TR,

Rest easy. There's nothing to worry about. Those are just Girl Scouts selling cookies.

A local diner has had too many accidents and wants all the flying projectiles to end. So, regardless what you do in your own home, if you eat out and have loose dentures please cover your mouth when you sneeze.

The American Medical Association is very concerned about the growing dislike people have for their doctors. They will conduct a survey to find out why the people dislike doctors. And if you want to take part in the survey, you can get a form from any doctor's office for three hundred and fifty dollars.

A reader writes:

Dear Ron,

Last night my wife and I were sitting in the living room and I said to her, "I never want to live in a vegetative state, and be totally dependent on some stupid machine, and fluids from a bottle. If it ever happens to me, I want you to just pull the plug." She got up, unplugged the television, and she poured my beer down the kitchen sink.

Another reader wrote saying:

"I moved to Hood River, Oregon, and they have a law on the books that says that you can't juggle without a license. So, I bought a license and I still can't juggle."

A reader writes:

Dear Ron,

Is there any significance to the weird names given to the months? For example, why is this month called October?

Signed, NT

Dear NT,

It's complicated. October was first called 'Germanicus' but nobody liked that name, so they changed the name to 'Antonius.' However, nobody seemed to like that either. Then someone said it should be named after a politician, so then they called it "Tacitus" after the Roman Senator, but before too long the opposing party opposed that name too. They changed the name a few more times. The other names included: "Herculeus" and "Faustinus." Eventually the politicians all agreed to take a more rational approach to naming the month. They decided to call it: "October" because it was the 10th month and "Octo" is Latin for 8.

FYI: This year on "Senior Citizen Day" at the Iowa County Fair, they hired extra help to stand around the bumpier rides to try and recover all of the flying dentures.

You may recall the reader who wrote to me last week, asking me if I had any good ideas as to how he could stop his wife from stealing the covers at night.

It now appears this is a bit more complicated than it first seemed. He wrote back to say that he forgot to mention that his wife sleeps in another room.

A reader writes:

Dear Ron,

Is it true that bugs can't see yellow lights?

Signed, BB"

Dear BB,

Yes, I think that is true, because when you are at an intersection, the insects seem to be totally unaware of flashing "Caution" lights.

A reader writes:

Dear Ron,

I read nearly 30% of the married women in the country have had extramarital affairs.

Is there a way to get those names?

Correction:

Last week we reported that Mr. Ernie Johnson was 111. That was wrong. What we should have reported is that Mr. Ernie Johnson was ill.

A reader writes:

Dear Ron,

The people who live upstairs have a big dog that barks all night and I can't sleep. What should I do?

Signed, CB

Dear CB,

In this troubled economy you should probably just be happy that you have a woof over your head.

Summer BBQ Tip:

When you barbeque, always put a piece of paper on the wall near the telephone, that has the fire department's number on it.

A reader writes:

Dear Ron,

For years I had headaches and was irritable and I had trouble concentrating, and then one day I began reading your column, and now I'm depressed too.

A reader writes:

Dear Ron,

Do you have any idea how I can keep my cat off the kitchen counter?

Signed, EH

Dear EH,

Yes, I believe I can help. You might try keeping the dog on the kitchen counter.

FYI: 1950s era, singer/song-writer, Don Gibson, has risen from the dead, reportedly to deny rumors that he is the father of actor, Mel Gibson.

FYI: A Sci-Fi program will air on TV next week about the enormous improvements in the quality of life on earth, after aliens land in a UFO and offer to give the earth people an unlimited supply of energy, and they show the earth people how to cure cancer, and they offer to vaporize Simon Cowell.

A reader writes,

Dear Ron,

I read Peter Minuit bought New York from the Indians for about 60 guilders, which is only about $24. Is that true?

Signed, WA

Dear WA,

Yes, I believe that is true. For what it's worth, I have actually been to New York and I bet that today it is probably worth twice that much.

A reader writes:

Dear Ron,

The other day I followed my wife through the department store for what seemed like forever. I wasn't sure if she was shopping or taking inventory. Is this normal?

Signed, Peeved

Dear Peeved,

You know what they say? They say that your wife is probably a shopaholic if the mall sends a limo over to pick her up.

FYI: Regarding the shopping habits of men and women, here's how it appears to work.

A man will pay $10 for a $5 item he wants and a woman will pay $5 for a $10 item she doesn't want but is on sale.

FYI: Once again this year many people were shocked and appalled at the nude beach on the Wisconsin River, near Mazomanie Wisconsin.

It is my understanding that quite a number of those people drove a considerable distance to get to that nude beach so they could be shocked and appalled.

International travel tip:

To avoid looking sick on a passport photo, have the photo taken <u>BEFORE</u> you find out how much the trip will cost.

Air Travel Tip:

If you want extra room when you are flying, you can usually get the person next to you to move somewhere else by merely asking that person if they would like to share some of your Beano.

If you're a new reader of this column, remember, nobody is perfect.

FYI:

I'm told that no husband has ever been shot while doing the dishes.

This just in:

A local man's home life was totally screwed up this week when the mail-order bride that he sent for 29 years ago, finally showed up?

There is a new religion where some women go around ringing doorbells, and if you let them in, they will serve you your dinner.

The religion is called: Jehovah's Waitresses.

To the reader who wrote wondering if banks will give refunds for lost traveler's checks:

Yes they will...normally. The exception would be an instance like...if you lost them in a poker game.

FYI: I learned an elderly Dodgeville couple is getting married. He is 87 and she is 85. Medicare is paying for the honeymoon.

A reader writes:

Dear Ron,

I ordered a book on mail order scams about three months ago. It still hasn't come.

Hold this page up to a mirror and read it in the mirror. You'll see it reads backwards. And if you then turn it upside-down and then read it in the mirror again, it will then read upside-down and backwards. However, there's one exception.

The word **CHOICE** is unaffected if read upside-down in a mirror. Try it and see.

A reader writes:

Dear Ron,

Since I started reading your column I have headaches, and I'm irritable, and I have trouble concentrating.

Signed, CD

Dear CD,

What a weird coincidence. I suffered from those very same symptoms until I started writing this column.

A reader writes:

Dear Ron,

I had a dream that I saw Elvis. He was standing in a haze. At least I think it was Elvis. It was rather hard to tell because of the haze. I wonder if you think this means that Elvis is alive?

Signed, JB

Dear JB,

From the haze you describe, I think Elvis is either dead and he is up in The Great Beyond, or he is alive and he's in Los Angeles.

A reader writes:

Dear Ron,

Even knowing the awful effects of smoking, many kids choose to smoke anyway. Is there anything we could do to stop this?

Signed, FB

Dear FB,

They probably need to try some psychology. They should make cigarettes out of broccoli.

A reader wrote:

Dear Ron,

I dated this guy and it started to get serious, so I took him home to meet my parents, and they liked him. Then one day we broke up and soon he started dating someone else. One day he brought her over to my house to meet my parents, and they liked her too.

Advice for those who are not street-wise:

If you find yourself on the street and you're in the middle of a gang shoot-out, the best thing for you to do is to find some way to get involved with one side or the other, because most gang related shooting victims are innocent bystanders.

A reader writes:

Dear Ron,

My wife refuses to wear a money belt when we walk the street on our trip to New York. She says it would make her stomach look too big. What do you think I should do?

Signed, LW

Dear LW,

Make her stomach look too big? In that case, I bet she would wear a money bra.

A reader writes:

Dear Ron,

Every year in Bristol Wisconsin they have a thing they call a "Renaissance Fair." What is a renaissance fair?

Signed, TR

Dear TR,

People at a renaissance fair escape reality by dressing up in costumes and they have lots of food, fun, and music. The best way I can explain it…it's like Mardi Gras, without the drunks.

A reader writes:

Dear Ron,

What are your beliefs about life after death?

Signed, BB

Dear BB,

You're asking the wrong person. At my age I don't even have much of a life after supper.

A reader writes:

Dear Ron,

I've been walking in my sleep. Do you have any idea what I can do to stop?

Signed, DS

Dear DS,

You might try wearing roller skates to bed.

A reader writes:

Dear Ron,

Last week your column had another typo. You had Dopeler Effect. The correct term is Doppler Effect.

Signed, TJ

Dear TJ,

Wrong. The Dopeler Effect is different than the Doppler Effect. The Dopeler Effect is when a bunch of stupid ideas tend to seem smarter because you tend to come up with them in rapid succession.

A reader writes:

Dear Ron,

Some people are ambidextrous, but my sister-in-law is aquadextrous. What is aquadextrous?

Signed, MO

Dear MO,

Aquadextrous is when she can lay flat, submerged in the bathtub and turn the faucet off with her toes.

A reader writes:

Dear Ron,

I keep finding a lot of typos in your column. Don't you have a proof reader at the paper?

Signed, TR

Dear TR,

I'm sure we have a proof reader at the paper, but I'm not sure who it is. I think it's either Curly or Moe.

Attention:

Because of liability problems, we may have to suspend our "Winter Driving Tips" if the readers don't start paying better attention to detail.

Last month, in the 'Winter Driving Tips' somebody thought we said, "Skid in the direction of your turn."

A reader writes:

Dear Ron,

I always believed that there's no such thing as a stupid question, but you sure come up with some stupid answers.

A reader writes:

Dear Ron,

I understand that Bill Gates is no longer the richest man in the world. What happened?

Signed, CB

Dear CB,

What happened is that Bill Gates now has kids in college.

A reader writes:

Dear Ron,

I hear the phrase, "The day the music died" quite often. What does that mean?

Signed, DD

Dear DD,

That refers to the day Buddy Holley died in a plane crash. However, there are a lot of people who think the phrase refers to the day Yoko Ono recorded her first CD.

A reader writes:

Dear Ron,

I wanted to start a small business, but I hear that three out of four small businesses fail. What do you suggest?

Signed, TK

Dear TK,

In that case I suggest you start a large business.

A reader writes:

Dear Ron,

I could never understand the difference was between the 'annuals' and a 'perennials.' Can you explain it?

Signed, WB

Dear WB,

An 'annual' you have to plant every year. Like: marigolds or sweet alyssums. And the 'Perennials' are something that will come back year after year for no apparent reason. A couple examples would be: Dandelions, crabgrass and 'As the World Turns.'

A reader writes:

Dear Ron,

Last month I wrote to you because I didn't know what I should call my mother-in-law. You suggested that I should ask her what I should call her. So that's what I did, and she said that she didn't care. She told me that I can call her whatever I am comfortable with. So that's what I did and now Gargantua won't even talk to me.

A reader writes:

Dear Ron,

Can this be right? I read the average number of calories in a piece of chocolate is 32 and the average number of calories that you burn while you're making love is 33. Well, if this is true, you could eat chocolate while you are making love and lose weight in the process.

Parenting tip:

Parents…consider NOT sending your kids to college. Just give them the money and let them retire.

If you recall, a reader had written to me to say his mother-in-law loves house plants and he asked if I thought it was okay to give her a palm tree for her birthday.

And I replied to the reader that I thought a palm tree would be too tall for a house.

Well, the guy wrote back to me saying that he thought it would be okay anyway, because his mother-in-law is now living in a light house with a cathedral ceiling.

If you're thinking that my column seems a little bit more incoherent today than usual, it's because I spilled a hot fudge sundae in my lap and as I write this, fire ants are crawling up my leg.

A reader writes:

Dear Ron,

It seems to me that I've seen it spelled both ways. Is the Italian designer's name Pucci or Gucci?

Signed, JW

Dear JW,

Pucci and Gucci are two different people. Pucci designed expensive underwear and Gucci designed expensive hand bags. However, at one point there was some talk about those two getting together, with a line of expensive baggy underwear.

A reader writes:

Dear Ron,

Do the islands of Samoa belong to England or the U.S.?

Signed, WW

Dear WW,

The English didn't want the Samoan Islands because they weren't sure where they were, so the U.S. ended up with them. My understanding is the Samoan Islands are an "Unorganized Territory," but not unorganized enough to become a state.

A reader writes:

Dear Ron,

This year I would like to try to grow my own cantaloupes. Are there any good books about cantaloupulation?

Signed, CB

Dear CB,

I haven't got a clue.

A reader writes:

Dear Ron,

You are getting up in age. I'm curious, which of your senses do you feel has diminished the most?

Signed, JM

Dear JM,

Probably my sense of decency.

A reader writes:

Dear Ron,

I read that TV audiences decreased by 8% in the daytime and 3% at night.

Any idea why that is?

Signed, WT

Dear WT,

I can think of a lot of stuff that the 3% might be doing at night, but I have no idea what those 8% are doing in the daytime that the other 5% aren't doing at night.

A reader writes:

Dear Ron,

I heard there is a $50 fine if you're caught spitting on a New York subway.

Do you think that is an excessive fine?

Signed, BJ

Dear BJ,

I think it probably is a little excessive, considering you can throw up for free.

A reader writes:

Dear Ron,

There's a survey that suggests married men are happier than single men, but the survey also suggests single women are happier than married women.

What's your take on that?

Signed, BW

Dear BW,

I suppose that's why married men prefer single women.

A reader writes:

Dear Ron,

Doctors claim that brandy can't cure the common cold. Do you agree?

Signed, MT

Dear MT,

It may be true that brandy can't cure the common cold, but on the other hand, neither can doctors.

A reader writes:

Dear Ron,

Most birds build their nests out of twigs, but swallows build their nests out of mud. Why is that?

Signed, Leonard

Dear Leonard,

The only reason I can think of is that mud is dirt cheap.

A reader writes:

Dear Ron,

How come they put your column buried in the middle of the newspaper?

Signed, PO

Dear PO,

The reason my column is tucked away in the middle is so that the other sections can protect it from getting damaged.

A reader writes:

Dear Ron,

I was wondering what percentage of the bank robbers are eventually caught?

Signed, Curious

Dear Curious,

Most bank robbers are eventually caught and I think there's a moral. If you want to take money from people, don't rob a bank. Open a bank and then the people will bring their money to you.

A reader writes:

Dear Ron,

I farm and I hate Daylight Saving Time, because when it is Daylight Saving Time, I have to go to bed with the chickens.

Signed, KF

Dear KF,

You're not the only one who is unhappy. Going to bed with the chickens makes the rooster mad as a wet hen.

A reader writes:

Dear Ron,

In my opinion you are despicable and your advice is about as useful as a sidecar on an exercise bike. Get a life.

Signed, Your mother

Correction: Last week we reported a record breaking javelin throw of 190 feet.

It turns out this was incorrect. The actual throw was only 150 feet. The guy the javelin hit crawled the other 40 feet.

A reader writes:

Dear Ron,

My husband and I have been married for 35 years and last month he decided that he was going to leave me. Then he read something in your column and he changed his mind and told me he is going to stay. Please cancel my subscription.

A reader writes:

Dear Ron,

Why did they name the Sioux Indian Chief Big Foot?

I think he should have been called Big Feet, not Big Foot, unless he had one big foot and one normal size foot.

And I guess that there's also the chance that he only had one foot, and it was big, which would make more sense, don't you think?

Signed, Puzzled

Dear Puzzled,

Let me think about that for a little while and I'll get back to you.

A reader writes:

Dear Ron,

I was the best man at a wedding last week, and the photographer was just about to take a picture when he looked up and shouted, 'Pull your stomach in.' I was extremely embarrassed, but then I realized that he was not talking to me. It turns out he was talking to the bride.

A reader writes:

Dear Ron,

I read in the paper that the Dodgeville train depot was built in the late 1800s and they built it a mile north of town. Why would they build it a mile north of town?

Signed, RL

Dear RL,

It's my understanding that they built it a mile north of town because they wanted it near the tracks.

A reader writes:

Dear Ron,

Every summer I have a real problem with those pesky Asian Beetles. What do you suggest?

Signed, DS

Dear DS,

No doubt your pharmacist can probably recommend a good shampoo.

A reader writes:

Dear Ron,

My wife and I have been married 32 years and for quite a while, when I come to bed, she acts like she doesn't even know I'm there. What should I do?

Signed, Frustrated

Dear Frustrated,

That is a problem. Try going to bed wearing blaze orange pajamas.

A reader writes:

Dear Ron,

I read that about three million years ago an ice glacier from Canada carved out the landscape in this part of the Midwest.

In fact, all of the rocks in this area were supposedly pushed here by that big glacier. But the article didn't say what happened to the glacier. Any chance you know what happened to the glacier?

Signed, SM

Dear SM,

My guess…it probably went back to Canada to get more rocks.

A reader writes:

Dear Ron,

Last week you used the word "irregardless" in your column. So you know…irregardless is not a word.

Signed, TM

Dear TM,

Irregardless of what you think, irregardless <u>is</u> a word which evolved from a blending of the words regardless and irrespective. Language is a living thing. In the future the evolution will include words such as "Irrepoluted," which is a blending of the words Erie and Polluted.

A reader writes:

Dear Ron,

You Bozos had 9 typos in last week's paper.

Signed, Norman

Dear Norman,

You may need to get your eyes checked. There were 13 typos last week.

A reader writes:

Dear Ron,

Do you know who it was that started the custom of the man having to give the woman a diamond engagement ring?

Signed, SC

Dear SC,

On that I'm not exactly sure, but I suspect that it was a woman.

A reader writes:

Dear Ron,

I notice that little girls always dress up in their mother's old clothes, but for some reason little boys never seem to dress up in their father's old clothes. How come?

Signed, GH

Dear GH,

Little boys probably don't dress up in their father's old clothes because their father is probably still wearing them.

A reader writes:

Dear Ron,

What is the best thing for a guy who is going bald?

Signed, TC

Dear TC,

If you are going bald the best thing is a sense of humor.

A reader writes:

Dear Ron,

I read that the best time to brush your teeth is before you go to bed. Why is that?

Signed, PN

Dear PN,

It's probably best to brush your teeth before going to bed, because it's so messy to brush your teeth after you go to bed. In that respect it's the same for going to the bathroom.

A reader writes:

Dear Ron,

Would you please let all of your readers know that any pre-nuptial agreement that was written on the back of a Hooter's cocktail napkin would not be binding in court?

Signed, SS

Dear SS,

You're the 4th guy to write to me about that.

A reader writes:

Dear Ron,

My wife is gone for three weeks and I have to do all my own cooking, and I can't cook. Any chance you have some advice for me?

Signed, CW

Dear CW,

Good luck. I do have one piece of advice. To lessen the frustration you might want to cover your smoke alarm with Saran Wrap.

Driving Tip:

If you are extremely tired and find you are nodding off while you drive, you can take the edge off, when you come to a stop light. Simply closing your eyes and take a short "mini-nap" while you are stopped at the red light.

You don't have to worry about knowing when the light turns green again, because when the light turns green again, the cars behind you will always let you know that the light has turned green.

A reader writes:

Dear Ron,

Could you announce in your column that there will be a great big Chili Cook-off in Downtown Dodgeville this Saturday?

Signed, Chuck

Dear Chuck,

You are really having a chili cook-off? Doesn't anyone care about the ozone layer anymore?

A reader writes:

Dear Ron,

I read an article that claims the human body produces millions and millions of new cells 24 hours a day, nonstop. Is that true?

Signed, BN

Dear BN,

I am afraid that is true. It's no wonder we have so much trouble trying to lose weight.

In an attempt to bolster ratings, CBS News will emulate what has made the primetime programs so successful.

In the future their news anchors will talk dirty.

Here is the answer to our trivia question

The trivia question was: Which celebrity was known as "The Little Tramp?"

The correct answer was: Charlie Chaplin. Several of you thought it was Madonna.

A reader writes:

Dear Ron,

Have you ever noticed that the nicest cars that are parked in the high school parking lot usually belong to the students?

A reader writes:

Dear Ron,

At work somebody said that he recently had to make an "O-Turn" when he was driving. What is an "O-Turn?"

Signed, FG

Dear FG,

An "O-Turn" is when you make a "U-Turn" and then you change your mind and go back the way you were originally going.

A reader writes:

Dear Ron,

I just heard that Fairchild Industries and Honeywell Industries will merge and will form the largest conglomerate of its kind.

Any truth to that?

Signed, EW

Dear EW,

Don't tell me….let me guess. Fairchild and Honeywell will merge and they will name the new conglomerate: Fairwell Honeychild.

Community Announcements

*If any of our readers are interested in a job working with animals, we have an opening here at the newspaper office.

*The Iowa County Sheriff's Department has just informed us that they are running out of speeding tickets. So if you want one you'll have to hurry.

A reader writes:

Dear Ron,

You seem to know quite a bit about the law. Did you go to law school?

Signed, SW

Dear SW,

I never went to law school, but over the years I have had the law explained to me by numerous judges and State Patrol officers.

A reader writes:

Dear Ron,

I wrote to you a week ago and I explained my situation and you suggested that, to save my marriage, the best thing for me to do is: give up drinking, gambling and running around with cheap floozies I meet in bars. What's the second best thing?

The reader who wrote to say his honeymoon was boring wrote back and explained that the reason his wife didn't go along on their honeymoon is because she had to work.

To the reader who wrote to me and didn't sign the letter: My advice for your unique problem is... Never, ever use acupuncture to relieve gas.

This just in:

The American Dental Association (ADA) reminds parents that they should limit the amount of candy they give to their kids on Easter and Halloween...

...and the American kids want the ADA to mind their own business.

A reader writes:

Dear Ron,

I heard that Shirley MacLaine claimed she was able to communicate with the dead. Was she just trying to get attention, or do you think she really could communicate with the dead?

Signed, Wondering

Dear Wondering,

You be the judge. She recently held a séance where she claimed to have contacted Elvis, and Jimmy Hoffa, and Abraham Lincoln.

She said Elvis told her he is still The King. Jimmy Hoffa told her he is still The Boss, and Abraham Lincoln just wanted to know how the play ended.

A reader writes:

Dear Ron,

I'm not sure I heard this right. I heard they stopped Milwaukee's Grand Avenue Mall from being put up for auction, and the mall will now be awarded to the winner of the State Lottery. Is there any truth to that?

Signed, CR

Dear CR,

You heard wrong. Remember: You can win some things, but you can't win a mall.

Dear Readers,

I always attempt to answer the questions that come in as best I can, but to be perfectly blunt, some of your questions are ridiculous.

For example:

Will they totally ban the cloning of humans, or will they just ban premarital cloning?

Do you think Bill Gates ever gets the urge to buy a lottery ticket?

If you own a business and the IRS takes you to court for cheating on your taxes, can you write off the cost of jury tampering?

If Boston is "Bean Town" why do they call Chicago "The Windy City?"

How come people who snore always fall asleep first?

Five things I can predict with certainty:

1. It is impossible to stick your tongue out and look up at the ceiling at the same time.

2. After they read the statement above, the really stupid people will actually try it.

3. Now it has dawned on you that you are one of the stupid people.

4. Now you're smiling 'cause you're a dope.

5. Even though you realize you are a dope, for some stupid reason, you are still smiling.

A reader writes:

Dear Ron,

Why is it, whenever you see an elderly couple, it's always the man who has the hearing aid?

Signed, Frank

Dear Frank,

You better figure it out for yourself, because I wouldn't touch that one with a 10 ft pole.

A reader writes:

Dear Ron,

I caught my wife out with a guy from work, then I caught her out with the guy next door, then I caught her out with a guy she used to go to school with. What should I do?

Signed, Frustrated

Dear Frustrated,

Don't worry. Your turn will come.

A young reader writes:

Dear Ron,

I have decided I want to be a comedian when I grow up. What do I have to do?

Signed, Jason

Dear Jason,

Be a comedian? When you grow up?

Make up your mind. You can't do both.

Regarding our story about the man who died after an ordinary sneeze…there appears to be more to that story.

It turns out he sneezed while he was hiding in a closet.

If you recall the reader who wrote wondering what keeps us from falling off the face of the earth, and I replied that we are kept from falling off the face of the earth by the law of gravity.

That reader has written again, this time wondering what it was that kept us from falling off the face of the earth before the law of gravity was passed.

A reader writes:

Dear Ron,

I just saw a television documentary about a female bull fighter in Spain. If you think any of your readers would like that kind of thing, I thought I'd write to say that I recommend it?

Signed, BN

Dear BN,

Are you sure that you've got that straight? As far as I know, there is no such thing as a female bull.

A reader writes:

Dear Ron,

A few months ago I gave a large donation to help a candidate who was running for office during the campaign. It was a "donation" but I wonder if there's a chance I'll get anything in return for my donation.

Signed, KT

Dear KT,

You've got to be kidding. Yes, you'll get something in return for your donation. You'll get a request for another donation.

Health tip:

The color of your food is very important. If the edge of your lettuce is brown and the edge of your steak is green, eat something else.

Did you ever wonder....

How come the Department of Agriculture keeps getting bigger and the number of farms keeps getting smaller?

A reader writes:

Dear Ron,

I'm okay now, but last month I was suffering from a rare form of amnesia called: Amour Amnesia. If you have it, you can't remember anything at all about your sex life.

It was horrible. Then it got even worse. I remembered.

Signed, BO

Dear BO,

And why are you telling me about this?

A reader writes:

Dear Ron,

I read with interest your comments about primetime TV last week. For some time now watching TV has pretty much eliminated any conversation between my wife and I, but that's the only good thing I can say about it.

If you recall a reader who wrote to say that her husband was a terrible speller and she wondered if I could offer any advice for him and I replied that whenever he was in doubt, he should check the spelling in a dictionary. She wrote back saying that doesn't work, because he's never in doubt.

A reader writes:

Dear Ron,

I don't know about you, but I feel that married men shouldn't have to remember every single mistake that they've ever made. I mean, there is no reason two people should have to remember the same stuff.

In some cultures couples do not go out together before they are married and in our culture couples don't go out together "after" they are married.

This month's Homemaker Magazine reports on a study that found the best way for women to remove dog hair from the couch is with a black dress.

~~~

Next week look for our fair and balanced, totally unbiased analysis of the ridiculous new Health Care proposal.

A reader writes:

Dear Ron,

Yesterday I met this guy on the street who was willing to sell me a $2,000 Rolex watch for only $50. My wife said it's not real. She thinks it's a fake. What do you think?

Signed, RW

Dear RW,

My brother-in-law got a similar deal once and a couple days later he asked me what time it is if the big hand is on the six and the little hand is on the floor.

A reader writes:

Dear Ron,

I just had some dental work done and I bet my crown cost more than Queen Elisabeth's.

Signed, PD

Handy Household Hint:

To get rid of ants in your kitchen you should sprinkle some sugar on the front room rug.

A reader writes:

Dear Ron,

How do you feel about foreign aid?

Signed, GJ

Dear GJ,

You mean, like when they transfer money from the poor people in rich countries and it ends up with rich people in poor countries? Don't get me started.

A reader writes:

Dear Ron,

I'm writing to remind your readers of the harmful effects of snack foods that contain hidden fats and too much salt and sugar, etc.

Specifically, they should avoid things like: Potato chips, pop, French fries, cupcakes, marshmallows, doughnuts, pork sausages, bacon, Twinkies, chocolate covered muffins, Sugar Pops, and custard filled sweat rolls.

Signed, TM

Dear TM,

Wow! What an unbelievable coincidence. That's what I had for breakfast.

Dear Ron,

This page was blank until I added this line.

A reader writes:

Dear Ron,

Here's a funny joke for you. "If you think your dog is dumb, just remember who is working to support it."

Signed, BN

Dear BN,

I hope you didn't write that while you were supposed to be working. Always remember, "The worst part about getting a new puppy is the paperwork."

Regarding the item in last week's paper where a woman hit a police officer with her car; we now find that there is more to that story. At the time of the incident the officer was off duty and he was at home soaking in his bathtub.

A reader wrote to say his boss has a big smile on his face first thing every morning and the only reason it's there is because his boss just wants to get it out of the way.

FYI: Boss spelled backwards is: Double-S O B.

A reader writes,

Dear Ron,

Do you have any idea why women close their eyes when they kiss?

Signed, JB

Dear JB,

That would be rather difficult for me to answer....unless you sent me your picture.

Most of the time readers write to me, but last night at about quarter to two in the morning, an intoxicated reader called me from a bar and said he was in an argument with another guy and he needed to know if the special theory of relativity and the general theory of relativity differ when it comes to things like: "The Clock Paradox."

I told him that it was not the kind of thing that could be explained over the phone at quarter to two in the morning. I asked why he couldn't have waited to ask that question at a decent time of day tomorrow morning. He said, "Because tomorrow morning I won't give a damn."

Advice for the handyman: The best time to fix something is when your wife tells you to.

A reader writes:

Dear Ron,

You had another typo last week. You misspelled the word Ebonics. You had Elbonics.

Signed, GB

Dear GB,

No, that wasn't a typo. Elbonics is a word. Elbonics is when two people sit next to each other on an airliner and try to outmaneuver each other for the center armrest.

A reader writes:

Dear Ron,

The science channel had a documentary in which they stated that there are more stars in the universe than there are grains of sand on all of the beaches in the world. I find that hard to believe.

Signed, DD

Dear DD,

If you don't believe it…count 'em.

Correction:

Last week we reported that the Iowa County Little League Baseball Team will travel to Chicago where they will visit with some of the Chicago Cubs baseball players to get some basic pointers about playing baseball. We should have said "give" some pointers about playing baseball.

Regarding the numerous letters to the editor:

Letters to the editor are difficult to read when you type them with your fists.

A reader writes:

Dear Ron,

I have fallen madly in love with a woman, but she doesn't even know that I'm alive. What should I do?

Signed, LS

Dear LS,

Mail her a copy of your birth certificate.

A reader wrote:

Dear Ron,

My fiancé has just told me that he wanted me to know that he has recently had a few affairs with other women. When I reminded him that he'd already told me that last week he said, "Well, that was last week..."

Signed, Becky

Along that same line: Another reader wrote wondering what must be done in order for his wife to forgive him if he was unfaithful.

Maybe I'm part of the problem. I told him that, in order for his wife to forgive him for being unfaithful, he first has to be unfaithful.

A reader writes:

Dear Ron,

The other day I heard two guys complaining and one guy commented, "If they live here, they should use English." Turns out they were not complaining about illegal aliens. They were complaining about lawyers using unintelligible legalese in legal documents.

Another reader writes:

Dear Ron,

Eventually every man begins to worry that he's not the man he used to be.

Not me. I worry that I'm not even the man I used to think I used to be.

A new study reveals that Prozac can help significantly for all of those PMS problems. Doctors now suggest that, at the first sign of PMS symptoms, Prozac, in high dosages, should be taken to reduce your misery until your wife feels better.

When it comes to NFL football, having the right equipment is very important. With that in mind, the NFL has recently developed the individually fitted game-day fan recliners.

A reader writes:

Dear Ron,

I don't fly that much, but when I do, I never know whether or not the guy next to me wants to talk. What is the best way to find out if the guy next to you wants to talk?

Signed, GW

Dear GW,

Don't wake him up to find out.

A reader writes:

Dear Ron,

I'm confused about wholesale increases and decreases. Can you help?

Signed, ED

Dear ED,

The difference between a wholesale price increase and a wholesale price decrease is pretty easy: The wholesale price INcrease gets passed on to the consumer.

Homemaker hint:

FYI: Grease stains can be removed from a silk dress with an ordinary scissors.

∼☉

Did you ever wonder why the word: "Phonics" isn't spelled phonetically?

A reader writes:

Dear Ron,

In these times I'd like to remind your readers…We were put here to serve others.

Signed, EW

Dear EW,

What were the others put here for?

A reader recently wrote to remind us that it was the American Statesman, Patrick Henry, who pointed out that, "Taxation without representation is tyranny." The reader said that, as far as he was concerned, taxation even with representation isn't all that great.

For history buffs: Patrick Henry also said, "Give me liberty, or give me death." And then, as they were just about to hang him, he fired his speech writer.

A reader writes:

Dear Ron,

My husband spends the football season watching football. If I knew more about the game maybe I could enjoy it with him.

First I'd like to know, what is the difference between college football and pro football?

Signed, PH

Dear PH,

The difference between college football and professional football is…in professional football the players get paid by check.

Correction:

In last week's classified section an ad stated: "Looking to marry an old man with lots of money and a big heart."

That classified ad was supposed to read: "Looking to marry an old man with lots of money and a bad heart."

Answer to our trivia question

Question: Who invented the first Norwegian car?

Answer: Henry Fjord

A reader writes:

Dear Ron,

On a recent trip to Dubuque I pulled over to get out of the way of a fire engine with its red lights and siren on. Later I noticed, when the fire engine drove back to the fire station, they still had their red lights and siren on. Any idea why they do that?

Signed, CC

Dear CC,

The reason that they also drive back to the station with their red lights and siren on after they have put out the fire is because, if they don't get back to the fire station right away, they tend to forget what's trump.

If you recall, a woman wrote a while back complaining that her husband can't drink and he can't play cards, and I replied that I thought she should be happy about that.

She has written again. This time to explain that she was merely trying to point out that he "can't" play cards and he "can't" drink, not that he doesn't.

To protect your teeth you should brush your teeth twice a day, and floss your teeth after every meal, and mind your own business.

A reader writes:

Dear Ron,

Shortly after moving from Chicago to Dodgeville I ran across a farmer at the hardware store and he was telling me about how smart his dog is. He said that he has twenty-seven cows and a large wooded pasture, and twice a day this dog goes out to that large wooded pasture and he will find every one of those twenty-seven cows and that dog herds them to the barn for milking.

He said one day last week he sold one of his cows and the next day at milking time that dog went out and brought back twenty-six cows to the barn and then went back out looking for the twenty-seventh cow. He said the dog went from the barn to the pasture and back so many times that he finally had to stop what he was doing and show the dog the check that he got for selling the cow, before that dog would stop looking for it.

Signed, MR

County Court Proceedings:

A local farmer was accused of stealing a pig from another local farmer. After deliberation the jury found the defendant "not guilty" but they said he had to return the pig.

The judge denied the jury's verdict due to the obvious inconsistency and sent the jury back to deliberate again. The jury eventually returned with a new verdict: "The defendant is not guilty and he can keep the pig."

In another court case involving an area man with numerous parking violations, the judge found the defendant guilty and told him, "Just because you went out and bought yourself a used UPS truck, doesn't mean that you can park any old place you want."

In another case the judge looked at the defendant and said, "Guilty or not guilty?" The defendant whispered to his attorney, "If he doesn't know, why should I tell him?"

A reader writes:

Dear Ron,

Enough is enough. Yesterday I finally confronted my husband because he clearly loves football more than he loves me.

You know what he said? He said, "But I love you more than I love basketball."

He is despicable. What I should do?

Signed, MR

Dear MR,

To offer advice I need more information. Has your husband given you any indication how you compare to baseball and golf?

If you recall, a high school age kid wrote to say that he won $10 playing poker and his teacher still thinks he's not doing very well.

I replied that I was pretty sure his teacher meant that he is not doing well "in school."

Well, that boy wrote back to let me know that...this was in school.

If you recall, I was contacted by a reader who was upset about the terrible economy and he was extremely afraid that it may never recover, and I recommended that he should try to think more positive.

He wrote back saying he has a more positive outlook about the economy now. Now he is positive the economy won't recover.

A reader writes:

Dear Ron,

My baby is starting to climb and I'm afraid that he will try to climb out of his crib and he'll fall on the floor and I won't hear him. What should I do?

Signed, Nervous

Dear Nervous,

If you're worried you won't hear when your baby falls on the floor…remove the rug.

A reader writes:

Dear Ron,

I'm having dreams in which I see talking mice and talking crickets and talking dogs and talking ducks. How unusual is this?

Signed, Concerned

Dear Concerned,

Don't be too concerned. You're probably just having Disney spells.

A reader writes:

Dear Ron,

The airlines are now charging more and are giving less. For example, they no longer give free meals, but they charge if you have extra luggage. You would think they could find some kind of tradeoff.

Signed, BP

Dear BP,

I agree with you. You would think they could do something. How about if they let the kids take a free ride on the baggage carousel?

County Court Proceedings:

In a recent heated court case the prosecuting attorney asked the defendant where he was on August 2nd, 2010. The defense attorney objected saying, "My client doesn't have to answer that question." The defendant said, "That's okay. I'll answer it."

The judge said, "Ask the question again." The prosecuting attorney said, "Where were you on the night of August 2nd, 2010?" Again the defense attorney jumped up and said, "I object your honor! My client does not have to answer that question." And the defendant again said, "That's okay. I don't mind. I'll answer the question."

The judge said, "Will you please ask the question again!" Again the prosecuting attorney said, "Where were you on the night of August 2nd, 2010?" The defendant said, "Umm...I can't remember."

A reader writes:

Dear Ron,

I think the honeymoon is over. Last night my husband got up and opened the window and said, "I hope it's not too cold for you." and when I said, "No, that's fine." he said, "I was talking to the dog."

Another reader wrote:

Dear Ron,

I was out watering the lawn the other day and from the neighbor's house I heard, "If you wanted someone who understands you, you should have married a psychiatrist."

A reader writes:

Dear Ron,

My husband calls me the "little woman" and it's getting on my nerves. What should I do?

Signed, VM

Dear VM,

Start calling him the "big mistake."

A reader writes:

Dear Ron,

My wife and I ate at a very unusual restaurant. They didn't have a dessert cart. Instead…the owner's daughter went from table to table selling Girl Scout Cookies.

Signed, WS

Dear WS,

I think I can top that. I ate at a restaurant that was so high class, one time a customer passed out and the maître d' wouldn't let the ambulance crew in the dining room until they put ties on.

A reader writes:

Dear Ron,

I'm writing regarding your advice last week. You said that it is foolish to leave large amounts of cash lying around the house.

It's not foolish. It's impossible.

As we end another year, I want to thank the newspaper's crack team of poof readers for doing there best to keeping this column nearly error free.

A reader writes:

Dear Ron,

Bad economic times seem to come in cycles. There was the panic of 1873, which took place in 1873, and the panic of 1929, which took place in 1929, and then there is the bad economy we are in right now. Which do you think was the worst?

Signed, RT

Dear RT,

It's hard to tell which of them was actually the worst. Perhaps the panic of 1873 was not as bad because it didn't affect new car sales.

A reader writes:

Dear Ron,

I'm having trouble getting rid of my old computer monitor. I can't put it in the trash. Nobody will take it. What do you suggest?

Signed, PR

Dear PR,

That is a problem these days. Probably the best way to get rid of an old computer monitor is to gift wrap it and leave it on the seat of your unlocked car at the mall.

And our last reader wrote:

Dear Ron,

Here's a good one for you. The prisoners at a maximum security prison were asked why they watch Soap Operas on TV. They said, "We thought it was part of the punishment." Top that if you can.

Signed, FB

Dear FB,

Yes, I can.

A woman who was found guilty of poisoning her husband is questioned by the judge. He says, "The poison you used in the coffee to poison your husband was so potent, one single drop could kill an elephant. What I want to know is if at any time you felt any remorse at all." The woman says, "Yes." The judge says, "When?" The woman says, "When he asked for a second cup."

A Serious Look at Humor

Humor is a funny thing. That isn't just an attempt to be cute. Besides being funny/funny, humor is strange/funny and it is in that sense that I was referring to it. The "Sense of Humor" is not understood by most people. People know that they like to laugh, and that's that.

There is something to be said for humor and the laughter that results from it. It's not frivolous. Humor can be more than mere entertainment. Humor has a way of uniting people. In fact I seriously recommend that someone should plant some whoopee cushions in the United Nations.

There is an attitude adjustment that takes place when you laugh. It is difficult to laugh with someone and dislike that person at the same time. Using humor properly can help you disagree without being disagreeable. It can help you to make a point, without making an enemy.

Too much of our daily dialogue is predictable. This causes the mind to wander when we should be listening. Humor can make listening fun as well as interesting. That's why it is used in TV commercials and by speakers and trainers. It takes many words to make the very same point that a political cartoon can make "at a glance."

Why Do We Laugh?

It's probably important to know why people laugh if you want to make people laugh. For that matter, it's nice to know even if you don't.

According to Robert Provine, "Laughter is part of the universal human vocabulary. All members of the human species understand it. Unlike English or French or Swahili, we don't have to learn to speak it. We're born with the capacity to laugh."

Babies laugh before they can talk.

Genuine laughter is spontaneous. Like blinking, blushing and sneezing, laughter is a response to a stimulation. It's not voluntary. While laughter can be suppressed, genuine laughter is not something you can do at will. Genuine laughter comes from within. It comes on its own. It breaks out. It's not something you choose to do.

On the other hand, a forced smile is different. Merely assuming that facial posture that we call "a smile" will generate a mild euphoria in most people. I'm not sure why this is. Try it.

Laughter is both physically and mentally healthy. Psychologists say that we need to take humor seriously.

What's It All About?

In his book "Laughter" Robert Provine says, "Laughter is an outgoing message we send to others. We are 30 times more likely to laugh out loud if we're with people, than if we're alone."

Laughter is universal. People may speak different languages, but we all laugh the same. That is… we all make the same sounds when we laugh.

How come people laugh if they are tickled? How come you can't tickle yourself? There are several theories that try to explain the laughter that results from being tickled. I'll leave it at that, but why can't you tickle yourself? No matter how ticklish you are, you can't tickle yourself, and that is worth talking about.

The reason you can't tickle yourself is because there is no surprise. With laughter, surprise is everything. If you tell a joke, the punch line needs to come as a surprise. The more the joke teller telegraphs the punch line, the more the listener sees the punch line coming, and the less laughter that is generated as a result.

In addition to the "Punch Line" every joke should have a "punch word." It's that key word that makes the joke funny, and that word should be the very last word in the joke. Even a word or two after the punch word will dilute the laugh.

Albert Rapp's Three Basic Jokes

Resisting suppression, Ridicule, Battle of wits

1. Resisting suppression is overcoming the stronger.
It is the reason people laugh harder when a politician, or an attorney, or a member of the clergy, or some other figure of authority, is the butt of the joke. It's the reason a joke was funnier to you when your high school classmate whispered it to you in the back of the classroom, when you were NOT supposed to be talking. Television news anchors now and then "lose it" and laugh about something while they are on the air delivering a serious news story and they are NOT supposed to be laughing. And in each case it's because they are resisting suppression.

2. Ridicule is overcoming the dumber or weaker.
Rightly or wrongly, ethnic jokes fall into this category, as do jokes that involve put-downs and ridicule. They give the teller a feeling of real or imagined superiority.

3. The battle of wits is overcoming the smarter.
This involves puns, riddles, word play and things like that. The teller is superior because he/she "gets the joke" or can "solve the riddle" or can "understand the pun."

There are five types of laughter

1. Laughter from a joke or something funny.
This also includes any laughter in anticipation of something funny happening.

2. Laughter resulting from being tickled.
When you're tickled you try to protect the area being tickled. This goes back to prehistoric times.

3. Contagious laughter.
This involves hearing or seeing someone laughing. The harder they laugh, the more you are likely to laugh. It's psychological. This is why they planted laughers in vaudeville audiences and why they use laugh tracks on TV sitcoms.

4. Laughing attacks or laughing fits.
Once these start they are difficult to control. i.e. News casters loosing it. Laughing in church, etc.

In his book "Laughter" Robert Provine, Ph.D. reports on a school that was closed for several days because of uncontrollable laughing fits.

5. Conversational laughter.
Conversational laughter isn't laughter at all. It is a kind of body language people use in conversation. We use it for emphasis or to make a point. Watch people in ordinary conversations. Notice how when people are talking, especially in groups, the one speaking will periodically add a short laugh sound and/or smile while talking, even though nothing funny is being said.

Going Too Far and Offensive Humor

There is a line you can't cross, but you need to get as close to the line as you can, without crossing it. The closer you get, the harder they laugh. It's the very nature of laughter as a response to humor. It's that "resisting suppression" thing.

In some countries and cultures "Political Humor" will get a bigger laugh than "Sexual Humor" because political suppression is more dominant than sexual suppression in that culture.

The problem is that the line that you cannot cross is different from place to place. As they say, "There is a time and a place." What will work with your best friends after work, may not work at all in the presentation you were asked to give at a corporation's annual convention banquet.

Remember that some people seem to actually look to be offended and they take great pleasure in demonstrating how offended they are, so even if they only make up 2% of the audience in a business setting, they are usually so vocal about it, you might as well offend the entire group.

If it's funny and told at the right time and place, almost anything goes, but if it's just crude, or merely an attempt to shock…don't bother.

Using Humor

1. Only a few people can tell a good long joke. There are some, but very few. Most people give detail that isn't necessary. The detail doesn't add to the joke, it detracts from the joke, and dilutes the laugh. So, as you would in a business letter, get rid of every word that's not absolutely necessary. Cut it down to the bare minimum.

2. There is a key word at the end of every joke. It's the one word that makes the joke funny and that word should be the very last word in the joke. Even a word or two after that key word will dilute the laugh.

Good example: I don't mind cooking for myself. What I hate is eating it.

Bad example: I don't mind cooking for myself. What I hate is eating it because it tastes so bad.

3. If you're using something new, even if it's an old joke, if it's new to you, it's not enough to mull it over in your mind, and try to deliver it out loud for the first time when you are in front of the group. There's a good chance you will trip on your tongue. So even if you feel foolish riding alone in your car, talking to yourself, say the words over and over, out loud, enough times so they flow smoothly, and they will flow smoothly when you get up in front of the group as well.

Exaggeration and Humor

One ingredient used in a joke is exaggeration. You either overstate the case, or you understate the case, but either way, you exaggerate the case. That is why humor works so well when it is used to make a point. Just as a magnifying glass makes things bigger and easier to see, the exaggeration in a joke makes the point exaggerated and easier to see, and more likely to be remembered as well.

Examples:
The doctor says, "Would you like the baby's father to be in the delivery room with you?"

The woman says, "No. My husband and the baby's father don't get along."

A salesman tells his boss, "I made 17 sales calls, and I could have made even more, but some of the people wanted to know what I was selling."

Nobody is that stupid, but the exaggeration in the joke makes the point you are trying to make, bigger and much easier to see. "It's not how hard you work that counts, it's how effective you are." Enthusiasm without effectiveness is known as: "Energized incompetence."

FYI…it *is* possible to over-exaggerate.

The Case For and Against Humor

I was waiting to board a plane in Philadelphia. Even in "The "City of Brotherly Love" an airport can be a cold place. People just quietly go about their business. In the hubbub of a busy airport, they are usually in their own little world.

A guy sitting a few seats away from me had just bought a soft drink and had taken a big swallow. It must have gone down the wrong way, because he started coughing and choking as a fine mist shot from his mouth and nose and dripped down his chin. Nobody actually got sprayed, but you can imagine the guy felt embarrassed about the incident because everyone's eyes were on him.

It was easy to have empathy for his predicament. As luck would have it, it had been raining that day and I had an umbrella. I grabbed the umbrella, opened it, and held it between me and the guy spewing his beverage. Naturally, this got a laugh from him, as well as from the other people who were in that gate area.

That simple action changed the mood by easing his humiliation and lightening the moment. People started to talk to him, to me, and to each other. The humor in this non-verbal umbrella gesture brought a bunch of total strangers together.

Humor has a way of bringing people together. Humor unites people, and I seriously recommend that someone should plant some Whoopee Cushions in the United Nations.

There not only is a place for humor in the work place, there is a <u>need</u> for humor in the work place. It helps employees to bond and work as a team.

Comedy writing guru, Gene Perret, says a discreet mixture of wisdom and wit produces likability. This by-product of humor helps salespeople and executives. People not only hear what is said with humor, they will remember it longer and better. The uniqueness of wit makes it memorable.

However, going back to that umbrella incident; my humor could have backfired. In this case I defended myself (from getting wet) with an umbrella and everything went well. But what if I had elected to defend myself with a squirt gun? What if I fought liquid with liquid. There is a real good chance that I may have been misunderstood; if not from the guy spewing his beverage, but by the security guards. Obviously, you always need to be careful with humor so it doesn't go too far.

I hope you enjoyed the book.

"The best things in life are silly."
– Scott Adams, Dilbert

"Humor is one of the most serious tools we have for dealing with impossible situations."
– Erica Jong

"My life has no purpose, no direction, no aim,
no meaning, but I'm happy. I can't figure it out. What am I doing right?"
– Charles M. Schulz, Snoopy

"A person without a sense of humor is like a vehicle without shock absorbers."
– Gerry Hopman

And expressed geometrically: "Laughter is the shortest distance between two people."
– Victor Borge

"My parents felt laughter was the best medicine, so whenever I got sick, they would just laugh."
– Henny Youngman

Other books by Ron Dentinger:

"Down Time"

and

"How To Argue With Your Spouse"

(with Rich Renik & Chuck Gekas)

Made in the USA
Coppell, TX
30 May 2020

26707408R00098